THE ULTIMATE BOWLS COOKBOOK

RECHARGE YOUR ENERGY WITH A COMBINATION OF EASY, QUICK AND NUTRITITIOUS BOWL RECIPES

Tasty Food Press

TABLE OF CONTENTS:

CHAPTER 1: BUDDHA BOWLS 7
- THAI CURRY NOODLE BOWL 8
- EGG ROLL BOWL 10
- EASY SWEET POTATO BOWL 12
- EGG BREAKFAST BOWL 15
- BUDDHA BOWL 18
- BROCCOLI CAULIFLOWER CHICKPEA BOWL 21
- FANTASTIC SUPER SUMMER KALE SALAD 23
- BACKYARD BERRY BOWL 26
- FESTIVE NUT BOWL 28
- VEGGIE BULGUR SALAD 29

CHAPTER 2: VEGAN BOWLS 32
- SPICY TOFU SALAD BOWL 33
- CAULIFLOWER SALAD BOWL 35
- TASTY ROASTED VEGGIE BUDDHA BOWL 37
- VEGAN QUINOA AND GUAC BOWL 40
- MEXICAN VEGETABLE RICE BOWL 43
- FAST BROWN RICE BUDDHA BOWL 45
- AVOCADO BREAKFAST BOWL 48
- ROASTED PUMPKIN SOUP BOWLS 50
- SUMMER IN A BOWL 54
- CHICKPEA BUDDHA BOWL 56
- VEGAN SMOOTHIE BOWL WITH CARROT AND BANANA 59

CHAPTER 3: POKE BOWLS 62
- SMOKED SALMON POKE BOWL 63
- AMAZING AHI POKE BASIC 66
- TUNA POKE 68
- SHRIMP NOODLE POKE BOWLS 70
- AHI SHOYU POKE 72

CHAPTER 4: BOWLS WITH MEAT 74
- AVOCADO-TURKEY RICE BOWL 75
- TASTY KOREAN BARBECUE RICE BOWL 77

GREEK CHICKEN COUSCOUS BOWL 79
BEEF AND RICED BROCCOLI BOWL 83
FANTASTIC MEXICAN TURKEY AND RICE BOWL 85
RAMEN BOWL 87

CHAPTER 5: SMOOTHIE BOWLS 91

SWEET POTATO SMOOTHIE BOWL 92
SMOOTHIE BOWL WITH MANGO AND COCONUT 94
OVERNIGHT OATS BLUEBERRY SMOOTHIE BOWL..96
RASPBERRY-COCONUT SMOOTHIE BOWL..98
EASY STRAWBERRY-BANANA SMOOTHIE BOWL..100
ACAI SMOOTHIE BOWL 102
BLUEBERRY SMOOTHIE BOWL 105
HEALTHY BERRY SMOOTHIE BOWL 107
AMAZING HONEY-KISSED SMOOTHIE BOWL...109

© Copyright 2021 by Tasty Food Press All rights reserved. The following Book is reproduced below with the goal of providing information that is as accurate and reliable as possible. Regardless, purchasing this Book can be seen as consent to the fact that both the publisher and the author of this book are in no way experts on the topics discussed within and that any recommendations or suggestions that are made herein are for entertainment purposes only. Professionals should be consulted as needed prior to undertaking any of the action endorsed herein.

This declaration is deemed fair and valid by both the American Bar Association and the Committee of Publishers Association and is legally binding throughout the United States.

Furthermore, the transmission, duplication, or reproduction of any of the following work including specific information will be considered an illegal act irrespective of if it is done electronically or in print. This extends to creating a secondary or tertiary copy of the work or a recorded copy and is only allowed with the express written consent from the Publisher. All additional right reserved.

The information in the following pages is broadly considered a truthful and accurate account of facts and as such, any inattention, use, or misuse of the information in question by the reader will render any resulting actions solely under their purview. There are no scenarios in which the publisher or the original author of this work can be in any fashion deemed liable for any hardship or damages that may befall them after undertaking information described herein.

Additionally, the information in the following pages is intended only for informational purposes and should thus be thought of as universal. As befitting its nature, it is presented without assurance regarding its prolonged validity or interim quality. Trademarks that are mentioned are done without written consent and can in no way be considered an endorsement from the trademark holder.

CHAPTER 1: BUDDHA BOWLS

THAI CURRY NOODLE BOWL

Prep:
20 mins
Additional:
10 mins
Total:
30 mins
Servings:
6
Yield:
6 servings

INGREDIENTS:

1 tablespoon peanut oil
2 cloves garlic, minced
1 (32 ounce) Infused Broth
1 large carrot, peeled and cut into 2-inch matchstick thin strips
1 (8 ounce) package wide rice noodles, prepared according to package directions
3 tablespoons sliced green onions
⅓ cup chopped fresh cilantro leaves
3 tablespoons chopped dry-roasted, salted peanuts
6 wedges lime

DIRECTIONS:

1

Heat the oil in a 2 1/2-quart saucepan over medium-high heat. Add the garlic and cook and stir for 45 seconds.

2

Add the broth to the saucepan and heat to a boil. Reduce the heat to medium. Add the carrot and cook for 5 minutes or until tender-crisp.

3

Add the noodles to the saucepot and cook until the mixture is hot and bubbling. Serve topped with the green onions, cilantro and peanuts with the lime wedges on the side.

NUTRITION FACTS:

210 calories; protein 3.3g; carbohydrates 38.3g; fat 4.6g;

EGG ROLL BOWL

Prep:
10 mins
Cook:
20 mins
Total:
30 mins
Servings:
4
Yield:
4 servings

INGREDIENTS:

1 pound bulk pork sausage
1 (16 ounce) package coleslaw mix
¼ cup soy sauce
¼ cup toasted sesame oil
1 tablespoon grated ginger
1 clove garlic, minced
1 tablespoon lemon zest
1 teaspoon chopped fresh cilantro

DIRECTIONS:

1

Cook and stir sausage in a large skillet until browned, about 10 minutes.
 Drain excess grease.

2

Stir coleslaw mix, soy sauce, sesame oil, ginger, and garlic into the skillet;
cook until coleslaw softens, about 8 minutes.
Stir in lemon zest and cilantro; cook until flavors combine, about 2 minutes.

NUTRITION FACTS:

509 calories; protein 17.9g; carbohydrates 16.9g; fat 41g; cholesterol 74mg;

EASY SWEET POTATO BOWL

Prep:
10 mins
Cook:
20 mins
Total:
30 mins
Servings:
2
Yield:
2 servings

INGREDIENTS:

2 teaspoons olive oil, divided
1 cup ground sausage
2 large Eggland's Best Eggs
1 large sweet potato
Salt and pepper
½ cup salsa
1 avocado, diced

DIRECTIONS:

1
Heat 1 teaspoon of olive oil in a medium pan over medium-high heat and brown the ground sausage, 5 to 7 minutes.

2
While the sausage cooks, fill a large pot with a few inches of water and place over medium-high heat until it just starts to simmer.

3
Crack Eggland's Best eggs individually into a ramekin or cup. Create a gentle whirlpool in the simmering water. Slowly pour the eggs one by one into the water and leave to cook for 3 minutes. Remove with a slotted spoon and drain on paper towels.

4
While the eggs poach, cut the sweet potato into noodles using a spiralizer.

5
Heat the other teaspoon of olive oil in a large skillet over medium heat. Add in the sweet potato noodles  and cook until they just begin to soften, about 5 to 7 minutes. Season with salt and pepper.

6
Transfer the cooked sweet potato noodles into a large bowl. Drain the ground sausage and add to the sweet potato noodles. Toss with the salsa.

7 Divide the noodles and sausage between two bowls, top each with diced avocado and a poached egg.

NUTRITION FACTS:

624 calories; protein 19.9g; carbohydrates 59g; fat 36.4g; cholesterol 218.9mg;

EGG BREAKFAST BOWL

Prep:
10 mins
Cook:
25 mins
Total:
35 mins
Servings:
1
Yield:
1 serving

INGREDIENTS:

12 frozen bite-size potato nuggets
2 eggs
1 ½ tablespoons salsa
1 tablespoon milk
cooking spray
¼ cup chopped green onion
¼ cup chopped green bell pepper
1 ounce grated Cheddar cheese
salt and ground black pepper to taste

DIRECTIONS:

1

Preheat the oven to 450 degrees F (230 degrees C). Spread potato nuggets on a baking sheet.

2

Bake in the preheated oven for 8 minutes. Turn potato nuggets and bake until crispy, 8 minutes more.

3

While potatoes bake, combine eggs, salsa, and milk in a bowl and whisk to combine.

4

Heat a skillet over medium heat and coat with cooking spray. Add egg mixture. Scramble until partially set, about 2 minutes. Add green onion and bell pepper. Cook until eggs are set, about 5 minutes more. Transfer eggs to a plate.

5

Place cooked potato nuggets in a large bowl and top with scrambled eggs and grated Cheddar cheese. Add salt and pepper.

NUTRITION FACTS:

436 calories; protein 23.3g; carbohydrates 28.3g; fat 28.1g;

BUDDHA BOWL

Prep:
10 mins
Cook:
48 mins
Total:
58 mins
Servings:
4
Yield:
4 servings

INGREDIENTS:

3 cups chicken broth
1 ½ cups quinoa
1 large sweet potato, diced
1 large red onion, diced
¼ cup olive oil, divided
kosher salt to taste
freshly ground black pepper to taste
3 cloves garlic, minced, divided
1 tablespoon minced fresh ginger root
1 pound skinless, boneless chicken breast halves
¼ cup lime juice

2 tablespoons smooth peanut butter
1 tablespoon soy sauce
1 tablespoon honey
1 tablespoon sesame oil
2 cups baby spinach
1 avocado - peeled, pitted, and thinly sliced
1 tablespoon chopped fresh cilantro
1 teaspoon toasted sesame seeds

DIRECTIONS:

1

Bring chicken broth and quinoa to a boil in a saucepan. Reduce heat to medium-low, cover, and simmer until quinoa is tender and broth is absorbed, 15 to 20 minutes.

2

Preheat oven to 425 degrees F (220 degrees C).

3

Spread sweet potato and red onion onto a baking sheet. Drizzle 1 tablespoon olive oil over mixture and season with salt and pepper; toss to coat.

4

Bake in the preheated oven until sweet potatoes are tender, 20 to 25 minutes.

5

Heat 1 tablespoon olive oil in a skillet over medium heat; cook and stir 2 cloves garlic and ginger until fragrant, about 1 minute. Add chicken and cook until no longer pink in the center
and the juices run clear, about 6 minutes per side.
An instant-read thermometer inserted into the center should read at least 165 degrees F (74 degrees C). Cut chicken into 1-inch pieces.

6

Whisk 1 garlic clove, lime juice, peanut butter, soy sauce, and honey together in a bowl. Whisk 1 tablespoon olive oil and sesame oil into mixture until dressing is smooth.

7

Divide quinoa among bowls; top with chicken, sweet potato mixture, spinach,
 and avocado. Sprinkle cilantro and sesame seeds
 over the top and drizzle dressing over each bowl.

NUTRITION FACTS:

799 calories; protein 39.8g; carbohydrates 81.9g;
 fat 36g; cholesterol 69.1mg;

BROCCOLI CAULIFLOWER CHICKPEA BOWL

Prep:
15 mins
Cook:
30 mins
Total:
45 mins
Servings:
5
Yield:
5 servings

INGREDIENTS:

½ cup cashews
4 cups broccoli florets
4 cups cauliflower florets
½ teaspoon garlic powder
salt and ground black pepper to taste
1 (15 ounce) can chickpeas (garbanzo beans), drained and rinsed
2 tablespoons lemon juice
1 tablespoon tahini
½ teaspoon salt

DIRECTIONS:

1

Place cashews in a bowl and top with water; soak until softened, 3 to 4 hours.

2

Preheat oven to 400 degrees F (200 degrees C). Line 2 baking sheets with parchment paper or spray with cooking spray.

3

Spread broccoli and cauliflower onto 1 baking sheet and season with garlic powder, salt, and pepper. Spread chickpeas onto the other baking sheet and season with salt and pepper.

4

Roast in the preheated oven until broccoli, cauliflower, and chickpeas are softened and cooked through, about 30 minutes.

5

Drain cashews. Combine cashews, lemon juice, tahini, and 1/2 teaspoon salt in a blender or food processor; blend until dressing is smooth.

6

Transfer broccoli, cauliflower, and chickpeas to serving bowl. Drizzle dressing over vegetables and chickpeas.

NUTRITION FACTS:

210 calories; protein 9g; carbohydrates 27.4g; fat 8.9g;

FANTASTIC SUPER SUMMER KALE SALAD

Prep:
20 mins
Additional:
4 hrs
Total:
4 hrs 20 mins
Servings:
8
Yield:
8 to 10 servings

INGREDIENTS:

¾ cup white sugar
½ cup vinegar
½ teaspoon salt
½ teaspoon ground black pepper
¼ cup extra-virgin olive oil
1 bunch kale, stems removed and leaves chopped
½ (16 ounce) package frozen shelled edamame (soybeans), thawed
¼ red onion, sliced thin
1 cup shredded carrot
⅔ cup fresh blueberries
½ cup sweetened dried cranberries
½ cup cashew pieces
½ cup shelled, roasted sunflower seeds

DIRECTIONS:

1

Whisk sugar, vinegar, salt, pepper, and olive oil together in a bowl until sugar is dissolved; set aside.

2

Toss kale, edamame, red onion, carrot, blueberries, dried cranberries, cashew pieces, and sunflower seeds together in a bowl. Pour about half the dressing over the mixture and toss to coat. Cover bowl with plastic wrap and refrigerate 4 to 6 hours. Serve remaining dressing on side.

NUTRITION FACTS:

44 calories; protein 9g; carbohydrates 41.7g; fat 18g; sodium 239.1mg.

BACKYARD BERRY BOWL

Prep:
10 mins
Total:
10 mins
Servings:
2
Yield:
2 bowls

INGREDIENTS:

1 cup ice cubes, or as needed
1 cup strawberries, divided
2 bananas, sliced, divided
½ cup blackberries
¼ cup apple juice
½ cup blueberries
½ cup granola
1 teaspoon honey, or to taste

DIRECTIONS:

1

Blend ice, 1/2 cup strawberries, 1 banana, blackberries, and apple juice together in a blender until smooth, adding more ice depending on your desired consistency. Pour smoothie into a bowl.

2

Top smoothie with remaining strawberries, remaining banana, blueberries, and granola. Drizzle honey over the top.

NUTRITION FACTS:

341 calories; protein 7.1g; carbohydrates 64.5g; fat 8.3g; sodium 15.1mg.

FESTIVE NUT BOWL

Prep:
5 mins
Total:
5 mins
Servings:
16
Yield:
4 cups

INGREDIENTS:

1 cup shelled pistachio nuts
1 cup dried cranberries
1 cup macadamia nuts
1 cup cashews

DIRECTONS:

1
In a large bowl, mix together macadamia nuts, cashews, pistachio nuts and dried cranberries.
Transfer to a nice serving dish.

NUTRITION FACTS:

175 calories; protein 3.6g; carbohydrates 12.2g; fat 13.8g;

VEGGIE BULGUR SALAD

Prep:
15 mins
Cook:
5 mins
Additional:
20 mins
Total:
40 mins
Servings:
6
Yield:
6 servings

INGREDIENTS:

1 cup fine bulgur
1 cup boiling water
2 tablespoons olive oil
1 onion, finely chopped
2 large tomatoes, finely chopped
1 cucumber, diced
2 green bell peppers, finely chopped
1 red bell pepper, finely chopped
7 green onions, finely chopped
½ cup minced fresh parsley
½ cup minced fresh mint leaves
1 teaspoon red pepper flakes, or to taste
2 tablespoons olive oil
juice of 1 fresh lemon
2 tablespoons pomegranate molasses

DIRECTIONS:

1

Place the bulgur in a bowl; stir in the boiling water. Cover and let stand for 20 minutes.

2

Meanwhile, heat 2 tablespoons olive oil in a skillet over medium heat. Stir in the chopped onion; cook and stir until the onion has softened and turned translucent, about 5 minutes.

3

Drain the bulgur and return it to the bowl. Add the cooked onion, chopped tomatoes, cucumber, green and red bell peppers, green onions, parsley, mint, and red pepper flakes. Drizzle with 2 tablespoons olive oil, the lemon juice, and the pomegranate molasses. Toss gently until the salad is thoroughly combined. Serve immediately, or refrigerate until serving.

NUTRITION FACTS:

216 calories; protein 5.3g; carbohydrates 30.4g; fat 9.8g;

CHAPTER 2: VEGAN BOWLS

SPICY TOFU SALAD BOWL

Prep:
10 mins
Total:
10 mins
Servings:
4
Yield:
1 large bowl

INGREDIENTS:

3 green onions, chopped
2 tablespoons soy sauce
2 tablespoons toasted sesame seeds
1 ½ teaspoons Korean chile pepper powder, or to taste
1 teaspoon white sugar
½ teaspoon toasted Asian sesame oil
1 ½ cups steamed Japanese rice
½ head of romaine lettuce (heart only),
torn into bite-size pieces
½ cucumber - peeled, seeded, and chopped
1 (12 ounce) package tofu, sliced

DIRECTIONS:

1

Mix green onions, soy sauce, sesame seeds, Korean red pepper powder, sugar, and sesame oil together in a bowl until evenly combined.

2

Place rice in a serving bowl. Toss lettuce and cucumber together and place onto rice. Arrange tofu over lettuce and cucumber. Drizzle sesame mixture over tofu to taste.

NUTRITION FACTS:

198 calories; protein 10.4g; carbohydrates 23.7g; fat 7.2g; sodium 471.8mg.

CAULIFLOWER SALAD BOWL

Prep:
15 mins
Additional:
4 hrs
Total:
4 hrs 15 mins
Servings:
8
Yield:
8 servings

INGREDIENTS:

4 cups thinly sliced cauliflower
1 cup coarsely chopped olives
⅔ cup coarsely chopped green pepper
½ cup chopped onion
¼ cup chopped pimento peppers
½ cup canola oil
3 tablespoons red wine vinegar
2 tablespoons lemon juice
2 teaspoons salt
½ teaspoon white sugar
¼ teaspoon ground black pepper

DIRECTIONS:

1

Combine cauliflower, olives, green bell pepper, onion, and pimento peppers together in a bowl.

2

Whisk canola oil, vinegar, lemon juice, salt, sugar, and black pepper together in a bowl until smooth; pour over vegetable mixture and toss to coat. Cover bowl with plastic wrap and refrigerate until flavors blend, 4 hours to overnight.

NUTRITION FACTS:

168 calories; protein 1.4g; carbohydrates 6.6g; fat 16g;

TASTY ROASTED VEGGIE BUDDHA BOWL

Prep:
25 mins
Cook:
42 mins
Total:
1 hr 7 mins

INGREDIENTS:

1 cup water
½ cup bulgur
1 sweet potato, peeled and cut into 1-inch cubes
4 teaspoons olive oil, divided
salt and ground black pepper to taste
½ pound fennel bulb, trimmed and cut into 1-inch cubes
1 small red onion, cut into 1-inch pieces
1 red bell pepper, cut into 1-inch strips
1 (8 ounce) package tempeh, cut into 1-inch pieces
½ teaspoon curry powder
2 teaspoons coconut oil

Orange-Curry Dressing:

¼ cup fresh squeezed orange juice
2 tablespoons olive oil
2 teaspoons red wine vinegar
½ teaspoon curry powder
¼ teaspoon salt
¼ teaspoon ground black pepper
2 tablespoons raw pumpkin seeds (pepitas)

DIRECTIONS:

1

Preheat oven to 400 degrees F (200 degrees C). Line a baking sheet with parchment paper.

2

Bring water and bulgur to a boil in a saucepan; cover and reduce heat to medium-low. Simmer until water is absorbed and bulgur is soft, about 12 minutes. Keep warm.

3

Place sweet potato in a bowl and drizzle 1
teaspoon olive oil over it; season with salt and pepper.
Toss to coat.

Transfer sweet potato to the prepared baking sheet, placing in 1 row. Place fennel in the same bowl, add 1 teaspoon olive oil, and season with salt and pepper. Toss to coat and place fennel next to sweet potato, keeping each separate.

4

Roast in the preheated oven for 10 minutes. Place red onion in the same bowl; add 1 teaspoon olive oil, and season with salt and pepper. Toss to coat and place on the baking sheet with sweet potato and fennel, keeping them separate. Place red bell pepper in the same bowl; add 1 teaspoon olive oil, and season with salt and pepper. Toss to coat and place on the baking sheet next to the onion.

5

Roast in the oven until all the vegetables are cooked to desired doneness, 10 to 15 minutes.

6

Place tempeh in a bowl and season with 1/2 teaspoon curry powder, tossing to coat.

7

Heat coconut oil in a skillet over medium-high heat; saute tempeh, turning occasionally, until all sides are evenly browned, about 10 minutes.

8

Whisk orange juice, 2 tablespoons olive oil, red wine vinegar, 1/2 teaspoon curry powder, 1/4 teaspoon salt, and 1/4 teaspoon pepper in a small bowl until dressing is smooth.

9

Divide bulgur between 2 bowls. Place half of sweet potato, fennel, red onion, and red bell pepper around bulgur; top each with 1 tablespoon pumpkin seeds. Drizzle dressing over each bowl.

VEGAN QUINOA AND GUAC BOWL

Prep:
15 mins
Cook:
30 mins
Additional:
10 mins
Total:
55 mins
Servings:
4
Yield:
4 bowls

INGREDIENTS:

1 (15 ounce) can pinto beans, rinsed and drained

Quinoa:

2 ½ cups water
2 cups quinoa
½ teaspoon kosher salt

Veggie Bowl:

1 tablespoon olive oil
1 red bell pepper, sliced
1 yellow bell pepper, sliced
½ teaspoon ground black pepper
4 cups lettuce leaves
1 cup vegan shredded cheese blend
1 avocado - peeled, pitted, and sliced
¼ cup vegan sour cream

DIRECTONS:

1

Heat pinto beans in a saucepan over low heat until hot, 5 to 7 minutes.

2

Bring water, quinoa, and salt to a boil in a saucepan and simmer until quinoa is tender and water is absorbed, 15 to 20 minutes. Remove from heat and set aside to cool, about 10 minutes.

3

Heat olive oil in a skillet over medium heat.
Add red bell pepper, yellow bell pepper, and black pepper; cook and stir until bell peppers are softened but still crisp, about 10 minutes.

4

Toss quinoa, pinto beans, and lettuce together in a bowl. Top with pepper mixture, vegan cheese, avocado, and vegan sour cream.

NUTRITION FACTS:

623 calories; protein 24.6g; carbohydrates 78.2g; fat 23.5g; sodium 846.2mg.

MEXICAN VEGETABLE RICE BOWL

Prep:
15 mins
Cook:
5 mins
Total:
20 mins
Servings:
2

INGREDIENTS:

4 teaspoons liquid amino acid divided
¼ teaspoon onion powder
1 large zucchini, diced small
2 large kale leaves, cut into 1-inch squares
½ (14 ounce) can coconut milk
½ cup raw macadamia nuts
¼ cup raw cashews
¼ cup nutritional yeast
2 teaspoons chili powder
1 pinch cayenne pepper, or to taste
1 pinch red pepper flakes, or to taste
1 teaspoon vegetable oil
1 cup hot cooked brown rice

DIRECTIONS:

1

Stir 1 tablespoon liquid amino acid and onion powder together in a small bowl to dissolve the powder into liquid; pour into a large plastic
resealable bag; add zucchini and kale and work the bag to coat vegetables
with the marinade. Squeeze bag to remove excess air and seal. Marinate vegetables for 10 to 15 minutes.

2

Blend coconut milk, macadamia nuts, cashews, nutritional yeast, chili powder, remaining liquid amino acid, cayenne pepper, and red pepper flakes in a blender until smooth.

3

Heat oil in a large skillet over medium-high heat. Pour zucchini and kale from the plastic bag into the skillet; saute just until heated through, 2 to 3 minutes.

4

Divide cooked rice between two bowls;
top each portion with about half the vegetable mixture.
Drizzle the blended sauce over the vegetables.

NUTRITION FACTS:

772 calories; protein 22.1g; carbohydrates 53.3g; fat 59.1g; sodium 468.8mg

FAST BROWN RICE BUDDHA BOWL

Prep:
30 mins
Cook:
18 mins
Total:
48 mins
Servings:
3
Yield:
3 servings

INGREDIENTS:

Rice:

3 cups water
1 cup long-grain brown rice
½ teaspoon salt

Dressing:

1 lime, juiced
2 tablespoons olive oil
1 tablespoon sesame oil
1 tablespoon dried Thai basil
1 teaspoon minced hot chile pepper

Vegetables:

2 tablespoons sesame seeds
½ (8 ounce) package snow peas
1 cup cooked chickpeas, drained
½ (16 ounce) package firm tofu, cut into strips
16 baby corn, cut into bite-sized pieces
1 cup grated carrots
1 small green bell pepper, diced
2 green onions, cut on the diagonal
2 tablespoons chopped fresh cilantro

DIRECTIONS:

1

Combine water, brown rice, and salt in a pressure cooker. Close and secure the lid; bring to high pressure according to manufacturer's instructions. Cook for 10 minutes. Release pressure naturally according to manufacturer's instructions. Drain any remaining water and transfer rice to a large bowl.

2

Whisk lime juice, olive oil, sesame oil, Thai basil, and chile pepper in a small bowl to make dressing.

3

Toast sesame seeds in a nonstick skillet over medium-low heat, stirring occasionally, until evenly browned and fragrant, about 5 minutes. Transfer to a bowl.

4
Cook and stir snow peas in the same skillet until bright green, 3 to 5 minutes. Remove from heat and let cool.

5
Arrange snow peas, chickpeas, tofu, baby corn, carrots, and green bell pepper over the brown rice. Drizzle dressing over the entire bowl; toss to mix. Sprinkle toasted sesame seeds on top. Garnish with green onions and cilantro.

NUTRITION FACTS:

583 calories; protein 18g; carbohydrates 80.5g; fat 22.6g; sodium 691.7mg.

AVOCADO BREAKFAST BOWL

Prep:
5 mins
Cook:
20 mins
Total:
25 mins
Servings:
2
Yield:
2 cups

INGREDIENTS:

½ cup water
¼ cup red quinoa
1 ½ teaspoons olive oil
2 eggs
1 pinch salt and ground black pepper to taste
¼ teaspoon seasoned salt
¼ teaspoon ground black pepper
1 avocado, diced
2 tablespoons crumbled feta cheese

DIRECTIONS:

1

Stir water and quinoa together in a rice cooker; cook until quinoa is tender,
 about 15 minutes.

2

Heat olive oil in a skillet over medium heat and cook eggs to desired doneness; season with seasoned salt and pepper.

3

Combine quinoa and eggs in a bowl; top with avocado and feta cheese.

NUTRITION FACTS:

372 calories; protein 12.7g; carbohydrates 24.1g; fat 26.8g; cholesterol 194.4mg; sodium 379.2mg

ROASTED PUMPKIN SOUP BOWLS

Prep:
15 mins
Cook:
51 mins
Total:
1 hr 6 mins

INGREDIENTS:

1 (3 pound) sugar pumpkin, halved lengthwise and seeded, or more to taste
cooking spray
3 tablespoons butter
½ cup diced onion
1 quart vegetable stock
3 tablespoons cornstarch
2 tablespoons curry powder
1 cup milk
½ cup sour cream
1 tablespoon soy sauce
1 tablespoon white sugar
½ teaspoon freshly grated nutmeg, or more to taste
½ teaspoon salt
½ teaspoon freshly ground black pepper, or to taste

DIRECTIONS:

1

Spray inside and outside of pumpkin with cooking spray.

2

Preheat an outdoor grill for high heat and lightly oil the grate.

3

Place pumpkin, pulp-side down, on the grate. Close the lid. Grill until tender, 15 to 20 minutes. Turn over, skin-side down; grill until pulp is very soft and lightly charred, 20 to 30 minutes. Reduce heat as necessary to keep the grill temperature below 450 degrees F (232 degrees C). Let pumpkin cool on the grill.

4

Melt butter in a large pot over medium-high heat. Add onions; saute until translucent and lightly browned, about 5 minutes. Add vegetable stock, cornstarch, and curry powder; bring to a boil. Cook and stir until thick and foamy and cornstarch is dissolved, 1 to 2 minutes. Reduce heat to medium.

5

Scoop pulp out of the pumpkin, reserving the hard shell to use as bowl. Add pulp to the stock mixture, breaking up any large lumps. Stir in milk, sour cream, soy sauce, and sugar. Blend soup with an immersion blender until smooth. Stir in nutmeg, salt, and pepper.

6

Reduce heat to medium-low. Cook, stirring constantly, until just starting to boil,
5 to 7 minutes. Remove from heat. Serve in the pumpkin shells.

NUTRITION FACTS:

326 calories; protein 7.7g; carbohydrates 40.4g; fat 17.4g; cholesterol 40.4mg;

SUMMER IN A BOWL

Prep:
20 mins
Cook:
1 hr 35 mins
Total:
1 hr 55 mins
Servings:
5
Yield:
5 servings

INGREDIENTS:

4 ears fresh corn
4 cups water, or more as needed
salt and ground black pepper to taste
6 vine-ripened tomatoes, diced
1 tablespoon butter
½ cup torn fresh basil
2 ounces grated Parmesan cheese

DIRECTIONS:

1

Cut kernels from corn cobs and set aside. Cut cobs in half and place in a pot with water and a pinch of salt; bring to a boil, reduce heat to medium-low,
and simmer until corn broth flavors blend, about 90 minutes. Strain broth and pour back into pot; discard corn cobs.

2

Stir tomatoes, corn kernels, and butter into corn broth; bring to a boil and cook until reduced and flavors blend, about 5 minutes. Season with salt and black pepper.

3

Stir basil into soup, ladle into bowls, and garnish with Parmesan cheese.

NUTRITION FACTS:

159 calories; protein 8.1g; carbohydrates 20.1g; fat 6.7g; cholesterol 16.1mg; sodium 244.8mg.

CHICKPEA BUDDHA BOWL

Prep:
20 mins
Cook:
20 mins
Total:
40 mins
Servings:
2
Yield:
2 servings

INGREDIENTS:

1 cup vegetable broth
½ cup red quinoa
1 ¾ cups Brussels sprouts
¼ cup cubed carrots
¼ cup peeled and cubed parsnips
½ red onion, chopped
2 teaspoons olive oil, divided
1 (15 ounce) can chickpeas, drained and patted dry
1 teaspoon ground turmeric

Dressing:

¼ cup tahini
2 tablespoons lemon juice
1 tablespoon maple syrup
5 tablespoons hot water
1 avocado, mashed

DIRECTIONS:

1

Preheat oven to 400 degrees F (200 degrees C).

2

Place vegetable broth and quinoa in a saucepan; bring to a boil. Simmer until quinoa is tender, about 15 minutes.

3

Place Brussels sprouts, carrots, parsnips, and red onion on a baking sheet; drizzle with 1 teaspoon olive oil.

4

Bake in the preheated oven until softened, about 10 minutes.

5

Mix chickpeas with turmeric in a bowl. Heat remaining 1 teaspoon olive oil in a skillet over medium heat. Cook and stir chickpeas until browned, about 8 minutes.

6

Mix tahini, lemon juice, and maple syrup in a bowl until well combined. Add hot water, 1 tablespoon at a time, until dressing is thin and smooth.

7

Divide quinoa, roasted vegetables, chickpeas, and mashed avocado between 2 serving bowls. Drizzle 1 tablespoon dressing over each bowl.

NUTRITION FACTS:

815 calories; protein 23.9g; carbohydrates 99.1g; fat 40.4g;

Vegan Smoothie Bowl with Carrot and Banana

Prep:
15 mins
Additional:
5 mins
Total:
20 mins
Servings:
1
Yield:
1 smoothie bowl

INGREDIENTS:

2 pitted Medjool dates
1 frozen banana, chopped
1 cup coarsely chopped carrot
½ cup unsweetened vanilla-flavored almond milk, or more to taste
½ teaspoon ground cinnamon
¼ teaspoon ground ginger

Topping:

2 tablespoons flaked coconut
1 tablespoon goji berries

DIRECTIONS:

1

Place dates in a small bowl and cover with cold water; let soak, about 5 minutes. Drain and chop.

2

Place chopped dates, banana, carrot, almond milk, cinnamon, and ginger in a blender; puree until smoothie is thick and smooth. Pour into a serving bowl.

3

Top smoothie bowl with flaked coconut and goji berries.

NUTRITION FACTS:

325 calories; protein 4.8g; carbohydrates 71.6g; fat 4.8g; sodium 215.9mg.

CHAPTER 3: POKE BOWLS

SMOKED SALMON POKE BOWL

Prep:
15 mins
Additional:
30 mins
Total:
45 mins
Servings:
4

INGREDIENTS:

¼ cup soy sauce
3 green onions, thinly sliced
1 tablespoon black sesame oil
1 tablespoon rice vinegar
1 teaspoon grated ginger
½ teaspoon garlic, minced
12 ounces smoked salmon, chopped
2 cups cooked brown rice
¼ cup diced mango
¼ cup diced cucumber
¼ cup diced avocado
¼ cup sliced fresh strawberries
1 teaspoon black sesame seeds, or to taste

DIRECTONS:

1

Combine soy sauce, green onions, sesame oil, rice vinegar, ginger,
and garlic in a bowl.
Mix until thoroughly combined.
Add salmon and marinate in the refrigerator for 30 minutes to 1 hour.

2

Divide brown rice among 4 serving bowls. Top with salmon, mango, cucumber, avocado, and strawberries. Sprinkle black sesame seeds on top.

NUTRITION FACTS:

283 calories; protein 19.8g; carbohydrates 28.5g; fat 9.9g; cholesterol 19.5mg;

AMAZING AHI POKE BASIC

Prep:
15 mins
Additional:
2 hrs
Total:
2 hrs 15 mins
Servings:
4
Yield:
4 to 8 servings

INGREDIENTS:

2 pounds fresh tuna steaks, cubed
1 cup soy sauce
¾ cup chopped green onions
2 tablespoons sesame oil
1 tablespoon toasted sesame seeds
1 tablespoon crushed red pepper (Optional)
2 tablespoons finely chopped macadamia nuts

DIRECTIONS:

1

In a medium size non-reactive bowl, combine Ahi, soy sauce, green onions, sesame oil,
sesame seeds, chili pepper,
 and macadamia nuts; mix well. Refrigerate at least 2 hours before serving.

NUTRITION FACTS:

396 calories; protein 58.4g; carbohydrates 8.6g; fat 13.7g;
 cholesterol 102.2mg;

TUNA POKE

Prep:
15 mins
Total:
15 mins
Servings:
4
Yield:
4 servings

INGREDIENTS:

½ cup low-sodium soy sauce
2 tablespoons mirin
1 tablespoon toasted sesame seeds
1 small shallot, cut into strips
3 cloves garlic, crushed
1 teaspoon freshly grated ginger
1 teaspoon sesame oil
1 teaspoon red pepper flakes
1 teaspoon sriracha sauce
1 pound sushi-grade tuna, cut into small cubes
1 avocado, chopped

DIRECTIONS:

1

Combine soy sauce, mirin, sesame seeds, shallot, garlic, ginger, sesame oil,
red pepper flakes, and sriracha sauce in a medium bowl. Whisk well. Add tuna and avocado; stir gently to coat with marinade.

NUTRITION FACTS:

273 calories; protein 30g; carbohydrates 12g; fat 10.9g; cholesterol 51.1mg;

SHRIMP NOODLE POKE BOWLS

Prep:
15 mins
Cook:
5 mins
Total:
20 mins
Servings:
2
Yield:
2 servings

INGREDIENTS:

1 (3 ounce) package ramen noodles (flavor packet discarded)
8 ounces frozen cooked shrimp, thawed
½ cup julienned red bell pepper
½ cup shredded carrot
½ cup thinly bias-sliced celery
⅓ cup bottled chile-lime vinaigrette
2 tablespoons chopped dry-roasted peanuts
2 sprigs fresh mint
1 pinch cracked black pepper (Optional)

DIRECTIONS:

1

Cook ramen according to package directions. Drain in a colander under cold running water until cool; drain again.

2

Toss together ramen, shrimp, bell pepper, carrot, celery, and vinaigrette in a bowl. Top servings with peanuts, mint, and black pepper. Serve cold.

NUTRITION FACTS:

299 calories; protein 26.9g; carbohydrates 16.6g; fat 13.9g; cholesterol 218.4mg; sodium 866.4mg.

AHI SHOYU POKE

Prep:
20 mins
Total:
20 mins
Servings:
4
Yield:
1 pound

INGREDIENTS:

2 teaspoons sesame oil
2 teaspoons toasted sesame seeds (Optional)
2 teaspoons finely chopped toasted macadamia nuts (Optional)
1 teaspoon grated fresh ginger
sea salt to taste
1 pound fresh ahi steaks, cut into small cubes
¼ cup soy sauce
¼ cup chopped Maui onion
¼ cup chopped green onion
1 chile pepper, seeded and diced (Optional)

DIRECTIONS:

1

Combine ahi cubes, soy sauce, Maui onion, green onion, chile pepper, sesame oil, sesame seeds, macadamia nuts, ginger, and sea salt in a large bowl.

NUTRITION FACTS:

191 calories; protein 28.4g; carbohydrates 4.4g; fat 6.1g; cholesterol 51.1mg;

CHAPTER 4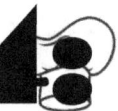

BOWLS WITH  MEAT

AVOCADO-TURKEY RICE BOWL

Prep:
10 mins
Cook:
25 mins
Additional:
10 mins
Total:
45 mins
Servings:
4
Yield:
4 rice bowls

INGREDIENTS:

1 ¾ cups water
1 cup uncooked basmati rice, rinsed
2 cups cottage cheese
2 medium avocados, cut into bite-sized pieces
1 cup deli turkey meat, torn into bite-sized pieces
4 teaspoons lemon juice
4 teaspoons soy sauce, or to taste
8 multigrain crackers
salt and ground black pepper to taste

DIRECTIONS:

1

Bring water and rice to a boil in a saucepan. Reduce heat to medium-low, cover, and simmer until rice is tender and water has been absorbed, about 18 minutes. Remove saucepan from the heat and let sit, covered, at least 10 minutes.

2

Arrange 1/2 cup cooked rice, 1/2 cup cottage cheese, 1/2 an avocado, and 1/4 cup turkey side-by-side in an individual bowl. Repeat with remaining ingredients to create 4 bowls. Drizzle lemon juice and soy sauce over each bowl and garnish with 2 crackers. Season with salt and pepper.

NUTRITION FACTS:

512 calories; protein 27.4g; carbohydrates 55g; fat 21.8g; cholesterol 34.1mg; sodium 1377.7mg.

TASTY KOREAN BARBECUE RICE BOWL

Prep:
15 mins
Cook:
5 mins
Total:
20 mins
Servings:
4
Yield:
4 rice bowls

INGREDIENTS:

1 (15 ounce) package beef roast in au jus
1 (8.5 ounce) package Rice
1 tablespoon vegetable oil, divided
1 (8 ounce) package button mushrooms, quartered
1 teaspoon Korean barbecue sauce
4 cups baby spinach
1 clove garlic, finely chopped
2 cups shredded carrots
1 teaspoon chopped fresh ginger root
2 tablespoons Korean barbecue sauce, or to taste

DIRECTIONS:

1

Heat beef according to package directions.

2

While beef is resting, heat rice as directed on package.

3

In a medium skillet, heat 2 teaspoons of oil over medium-high heat. Cook and stir mushrooms for 3 to 4 minutes; transfer to a medium bowl. Stir in 1 teaspoon barbecue sauce. Keep warm.

4

In the same skillet, heat spinach, garlic, and 1 tablespoon water for 1 minute or until spinach is bright green and reduced in size. Transfer to a serving bowl; keep warm.

5

Add remaining 1 teaspoon oil to the skillet. Cook and stir carrots and ginger over medium-high heat for 1 minute or until carrots are crisp-tender. Transfer to a serving bowl; keep warm.

6

Cut beef into smaller pieces. Divide all ingredients among 4 bowls; drizzle with additional Korean barbecue sauce.

NUTRITION FACTS:

352 calories; protein 25.8g; carbohydrates 36.8g; fat 11.8g; cholesterol 57mg; sodium 565.7mg.

GREEK CHICKEN COUSCOUS BOWL

Prep:
35 mins
Cook:
15 mins
Additional:
5 mins
Total:
55 mins

INGREDIENTS:

Chicken:

½ teaspoon dried rosemary
½ teaspoon ground black pepper
½ teaspoon salt
½ teaspoon dried oregano
½ teaspoon garlic powder
½ teaspoon onion powder
⅛ teaspoon ground cardamom
¼ teaspoon ground coriander
2 skinless, boneless chicken breasts
2 tablespoons vegetable oil
½ lemon, juiced

Couscous:

1 ½ cups water
1 cup dry couscous

Tzatziki Sauce:

½ cucumber, peeled and shredded
½ cup sour cream
½ cup Greek yogurt
½ lemon, juiced
1 tablespoon olive oil
1 clove garlic, minced
1 teaspoon chopped fresh mint
1 teaspoon chopped fresh dill
½ teaspoon salt
½ teaspoon black pepper

Toppings:

1 broccoli crown, cut into florets
1 medium red onion, diced
½ cucumber, peeled and diced
2 roma tomatoes, diced
½ cup chopped Kalamata olives, or to taste
½ cup chopped fresh parsley
1 (4 ounce) package crumbled feta cheese, or to taste

DIRECTIONS:

1

Mix rosemary, black pepper, salt, oregano, garlic powder, onion powder, cardamom, and coriander together in a small bowl. Place chicken on a plate and season with spice mixture. Heat vegetable oil in a saucepan over medium heat until it starts to shimmer, 2 to 3 minutes. Add seasoned chicken to the pan and cook, covered, 4 to 5 minutes. Flip chicken over and cook, uncovered, until browned on the outside and no longer pink on the inside, 5 to 6 minutes more. An instant-read thermometer inserted into the center should read at least 165 degrees F (74 degrees C). Squeeze lemon juice over chicken and allow to cool 5 minutes. Slice into strips.

2

While chicken cooks, bring water to a boil in a saucepan and add salt to taste. Add couscous, stir once, and cover. Remove saucepan from heat and let couscous steam for 5 minutes. Fluff with a fork.

3

Mix cucumber, sour cream, yogurt, lemon juice, olive oil, garlic, mint, dill, salt, and black pepper together
in a bowl until tzatziki sauce is just combined.

4

Divide cooked couscous between 4 bowls. Top with cooked chicken, tzatziki sauce, broccoli, onion, cucumber, tomatoes, olives, parsley, and feta cheese. Serve immediately or store in airtight containers to reheat later.

NUTRITION FACTS:

622 calories; protein 24.6g; carbohydrates 55.5g; fat 35g; cholesterol 75.7mg;

BEEF AND RICED BROCCOLI BOWL

Prep:
15 mins
Cook:
15 mins
Total:
30 mins

INGREDIENTS:

½ cup beef broth
¼ cup hoisin sauce
2 tablespoons reduced-sodium soy sauce
2 tablespoons sesame oil, divided
1 tablespoon oyster sauce
1 tablespoon cornstarch
1 teaspoon brown sugar
1 ¼ pounds New York strip steak, thinly sliced into bite-sized pieces
2 tablespoons butter
2 (10 ounce) bags frozen broccoli rice
1 teaspoon minced garlic
1 teaspoon salt
½ teaspoon ground black pepper
1 teaspoon toasted sesame seeds, or to taste (Optional)
⅛ teaspoon red pepper flakes, or to taste (Optional)

DIRECTIONS:

1

Whisk together beef broth, hoisin sauce, soy sauce, 1 tablespoon sesame oil, oyster sauce, cornstarch, and brown sugar in a bowl until cornstarch and sugar are dissolved.

2

Place sliced steak in a separate bowl and drizzle with remaining 1 tablespoon of sesame oil. Stir until evenly coated.

3

Melt butter in a large skillet over medium-high heat. Add broccoli rice, garlic, salt, and pepper. Cook for 5 minutes; stirring occasionally. Divide broccoli rice into serving bowls.

4

Add beef to the skillet. Cook over medium-high heat, stirring continually, for 5 minutes. Pour sauce over beef and cook for 5 more minutes or until sauce has thickened.

5

Spoon beef over broccoli rice.
Garnish with sesame seeds and crushed red pepper.

NUTRITION FACTS:

452 calories; protein 36.6g; carbohydrates 20.7g; fat 25.4g; cholesterol 100.1mg; sodium 2391.4mg.

FANTASTIC MEXICAN TURKEY AND RICE BOWL

Prep:
15 mins
Cook:
20 mins
Total:
35 mins

INGREDIENTS:

2 cups water
2 cups instant rice
olive oil
1 cup chopped red bell pepper
1 cup chopped green bell pepper
¼ teaspoon minced garlic
1 pound ground turkey
1 (15 ounce) can dark red kidney beans, drained and rinsed
1 (15 ounce) can tomato sauce
½ (14.5 ounce) can diced tomatoes
½ tablespoon chili powder, or more to taste
1 teaspoon garlic powder
1 teaspoon ground cumin
salt and ground black pepper to taste

DIRECTIONS:

1

Stir water and rice together in a microwave-safe bowl.
Cover and cook in the microwave on high for 8 minutes.
Remove from the microwave,
wait until water is fully absorbed, about 5 minutes, then fluff with a fork.

2

While rice is cooking, heat a large skillet over medium-high heat. Pour in just enough olive oil to coat the skillet. Add both bell peppers and garlic. Cook, stirring every so often, until the peppers are no longer hard and crunchy, about 10 minutes. Transfer peppers to a bowl.

3

Add ground turkey to the skillet and reduce heat to medium. Cook turkey, crumbling it up as you stir, until no longer pink, 7 to 10 minutes. Add cooked peppers, kidney beans, tomato sauce, diced tomatoes, chili powder, garlic powder, cumin, salt, and pepper to the skillet. Mix until everything is incorporated and heated through. Serve over rice.

NUTRITION FACTS:

414 calories; protein 27.9g; carbohydrates 52.6g; fat 10.4g; cholesterol 66.9mg; sodium 784.9mg.

RAMEN BOWL

Prep:
30 mins
Cook:
1 hr
Total:
1 hr 30 mins
Servings:
4

INGREDIENTS:

Broth Base:

8 cups water
8 cloves garlic, peeled and whole
8 slices fresh ginger root
½ medium onion, halved and separated
4 eggs
1 pinch salt and freshly ground black pepper to taste

Broth Ingredients:

½ cup soy sauce
¼ cup sake
2 tablespoons Thai-style chile sauce
2 teaspoons sesame oil
2 tablespoons white sugar
1 ½ teaspoons salt (Optional)

Finishing Touches:

15 ounces dried Japanese-style noodles
12 large shrimp, shelled and deveined, at room temperature
4 large dry sea scallops, halved, at room temperature
1 ½ cups fresh bean sprouts
½ cup sliced scallions

DIRECTIONS:

1

Combine water, garlic, ginger, and onion in a large stock pot and bring broth base to a simmer. Reduce heat to maintain an easy simmer for 40 minutes.

2

While broth simmers, fill a saucepan with water. Bring to a boil and reduce heat to a simmer. Lower eggs into the water 1 at a time. Cook 7 minutes for barely set yolks. Remove eggs from hot water, run under cold water until cool, and peel. Halve eggs lengthwise, place on a plate, and season with salt and pepper.

3

Fill a large pot with water and bring
to a boil in preparation for cooking noodles.
Reduce heat to a simmer.

4

Use a slotted spoon or long-handled strainer to remove garlic, ginger, and onion from the broth in the stock pot after it has simmered 40 minutes. Discard vegetables. Add soy sauce, sake, chile sauce, sesame oil, sugar, and salt and stir well. Cover stock pot loosely and simmer 10 to 20 minutes more.

5

Return simmering water to a boil. Add noodles and return to a boil. Cook noodles uncovered, stirring occasionally, until noodles are tender yet firm to the bite, 1 to 3 minutes. Drain and divide noodles between 4 large bowls.

6

Add shrimp and scallops to the simmering broth. Cook until opaque, 3 to 5 minutes.

7

Ladle finished broth into bowls to barely cover noodles. Add equal amounts of shrimp and 1 scallop to the center of each bowl. Place a portion of bean sprouts on the side of each bowl. Place 2 soft-boiled egg halves, yolks up, resting on noodles in each bowl; keep eggs above the broth. Garnish each bowl with scallions.

NUTRITION FACTS:

325 calories; protein 25.6g; carbohydrates 28.3g;
fat 10.6g;
cholesterol 233.1mg;

CHAPTER 5: SMOOTHIE BOWLS

SWEET POTATO SMOOTHIE BOWL

Prep:
5 mins
Total:
5 mins
Servings:
8
Yield:
8 servings

INGREDIENTS:

1 (15 ounce) Cut Sweet Potatoes in Syrup, drained
1 (6 ounce) container nonfat plain yogurt
1 tablespoon fresh orange juice
1 teaspoon organic honey
1 kiwi fruit, peeled and sliced
½ banana, peeled and sliced
⅓ cup fresh blueberries
¼ cup roasted sunflower seeds
¼ cup golden raisins

DIRECTIONS:

1

Place Bruce's Yam Cut Sweet Potatoes, yogurt, orange juice and honey in a power blender and process until smooth.

2

Transfer to a cereal or pasta bowl(s) and arrange kiwi, banana, blueberries, sunflower seeds and golden raisins over the top.

NUTRITION FACTS:

142 calories; protein 2.5g; carbohydrates 27.3g; fat 2.8g; cholesterol 1.3mg; sodium 35.7mg.

SMOOTHIE BOWL WITH MANGO AND COCONUT

Prep:
10 mins
Total:
10 mins
Servings:
1
Yield:
1 smoothie bowl

INGREDIENTS:

1 ½ cups frozen mango chunks
1 cup vanilla-flavored almond milk
1 frozen banana, chopped
1 tablespoon unsweetened coconut cream
¼ teaspoon vanilla extract
1 tablespoon flaked coconut
1 teaspoon goji berries
½ teaspoon chia seeds

DIRECTIONS:

1

Place mango chunks, almond milk, banana, coconut cream, and vanilla extract in a blender; puree until smoothie is thick and smooth.
Pour into a serving bowl.

2

Top smoothie bowl with flaked coconut, goji berries, and chia seeds.

NUTRITION FACTS:

443 calories; protein 4.5g; carbohydrates 90.3g; fat 10.6g; sodium 181.3mg.

OVERNIGHT OATS BLUEBERRY SMOOTHIE BOWL

Prep:
10 mins
Additional:
8 hrs
Total:
8 hrs 10 mins
Servings:
2
Yield:
2 bowls

INGREDIENTS:

1 cup rolled oats
1 ¼ cups unsweetened vanilla-flavored almond milk, divided
1 frozen banana, chopped
1 cup blueberries
1 teaspoon vanilla extract
1 teaspoon maple syrup, or to taste

Topping:

2 tablespoons flaked coconut
1 tablespoon fresh blueberries
1 teaspoon chia seeds

DIRECTIONS:

1

Combine oats and 2/3 cup almond milk in a bowl; refrigerate until oats have absorbed the liquid, 8 hours to overnight.

2

Combine oats-almond milk mixture, remaining almond milk, banana, 1 cup blueberries, vanilla extract, and maple syrup in a blender; blend until smooth.

3

Pour smoothie into 2 bowls and top with coconut, 1 tablespoon blueberries, and chia seeds.

NUTRITION FACTS:

354 calories; protein 7.6g; carbohydrates 68.7g; fat 6.5g; sodium 118.4mg.

RASPBERRY-COCONUT SMOOTHIE BOWL

Prep:
5 mins
Total:
5 mins
Servings:
1
Yield:
1 serving

INGREDIENTS:

1 large frozen banana
1 cup frozen raspberries
¾ cup unsweetened almond-coconut milk blend
2 (1 gram) packets Stevia In The Raw®
1 tablespoon coconut oil
½ teaspoon vanilla extract

Toppings:

Fresh raspberries
Flaked coconut
Chia seeds

DIRECTIONS:

1

In a blender, combine banana, raspberries, almond-coconut milk, stevia,

coconut oil,

and vanilla. Blend until smooth, adding a little more milk if needed.

2

Pour smoothie into a bowl and top with berries, coconut, and chia seeds.

NUTRITION FACTS:

588 calories; protein 4.8g; carbohydrates 104.8g; fat 20.1g; sodium 137.8mg.

EASY STRAWBERRY-BANANA SMOOTHIE BOWL

Prep:
5 mins
Total:
5 mins
Servings:
1
Yield:
1 serving

INGREDIENTS:

1 frozen banana, cut into chunks
1 cup strawberries, chopped

Topping:

½ tablespoon unsweetened coconut flakes
1 teaspoon chia seeds
¼ banana, sliced
2 strawberries, chopped
2 tablespoons fresh blueberries

DIRECTONS:

1

Defrost banana chunks for 5 minutes.
Combine banana and 1 cup strawberries in a blender; blend until smooth.
Pour into a bowl.

2

Top with coconut flakes, chia seeds, fresh banana slices, strawberry pieces, and blueberries.

NUTRITION FACTS:

238 calories; protein 3.6g; carbohydrates 53.6g; fat 3.8g; sodium 5.1mg.

ACAI SMOOTHIE BOWL

Prep:
10 mins
Total:
10 mins
Servings:
1
Yield:
1 bowl

INGREDIENTS:

1 large banana, divided
3 ½ ounces acai berry pulp, frozen, unsweetened
2 tablespoons soy milk, or more as needed
2 tablespoons granola

DIRECTIONS:

1
Combine acai pulp, 2/3 of the banana, and 2 tablespoons of soy milk in a blender; blend until smooth, but still thick. Add more soy milk as needed; smoothie should have the consistency of frozen yogurt.

2
Slice the remaining banana. Pour thick smoothie into a bowl and top with granola and sliced bananas.

NUTRITION FACTS:

282 calories; protein 4.8g; carbohydrates 45.1g; fat 9.6g; sodium 45.7mg.

BLUEBERRY SMOOTHIE BOWL

Prep:
10 mins
Total:
10 mins
Servings:
1
Yield:
1 smoothie bowl

INGREDIENTS:

Smoothie:

1 cup frozen blueberries
½ banana
2 tablespoons water
1 tablespoon cashew butter
1 teaspoon vanilla extract

Toppings:

½ banana, sliced
1 tablespoon sliced almonds
1 tablespoon unsweetened shredded coconut

DIRECTIONS:

1

Blend blueberries, 1/2 banana, water, cashew butter, and vanilla extract together in a blender until smooth; pour into a bowl.

2

Top smoothie with sliced banana, almonds, and coconut.

NUTRITION FACTS:

368 calories; protein 6.8g; carbohydrates 55.4g; fat 15.6g; sodium 8.5mg.

HEALTHY BERRY SMOOTHIE BOWL

Prep:
10 mins
Total:
10 mins

INGREDIENTS:

Smoothie:

1 cup frozen strawberries
1 cup frozen pineapple chunks
1 cup plain Greek yogurt
½ cup coconut water
2 tablespoons frozen acai berry pulp, or as desired

Toppings:

1 kiwi, peeled and sliced
½ banana, sliced
½ cup fresh blueberries
½ cup fresh raspberries
2 tablespoons sliced almonds
2 tablespoons granola
1 teaspoon chia seeds (Optional)

DIRECTIONS:

1

Blend strawberries, pineapple, yogurt, coconut water, and acai pulp in a blender until smooth; pour into a bowl. Top smoothie with kiwi, banana, blueberries, raspberries, almonds, granola, and chia seeds.

NUTRITION FACTS:

394 calories; protein 11.2g; carbohydrates 54.4g; fat 16.8g; cholesterol 22.5mg; sodium 138.2mg.

AMAZING HONEY-KISSED SMOOTHIE BOWL

Servings:
1
Yield:
1 serving

INGREDIENTS:

Smoothie:

1 frozen banana
1 cup almond, soy, or dairy milk
3 tablespoons almond butter or natural peanut butter
½ teaspoon vanilla extract
2 tablespoons Aunt Sue's® Raw & Unfiltered Honey
¼ cup coconut milk
¼ cup dark chocolate chips
½ cup ice

Toppings:

Assorted berries
Shredded coconut
Prepared granola
Assorted chopped nuts

DIRECTIONS:

1
Combine all smoothie ingredients into a blender. Blend until smooth.

2
Remove and pour into a bowl.

3
Garnish with assorted toppings. Enjoy!

NUTRITION FACTS:

952 calories; protein 11.7g; carbohydrates 112.9g; fat 57.5g; sodium 398.1mg

www.ingramcontent.com/pod-product-compliance
Lightning Source LLC
Chambersburg PA
CBHW070931080526
44589CB00013B/1472